D1274392

E-SPORTS AND THE WORLD OF
COMPETITIVE
GAMING

By Heather L. Bode

**ReferencePoint
Press®**

San Diego, CA

© 2019 ReferencePoint Press, Inc.
Printed in the United States

For more information, contact:
ReferencePoint Press, Inc.
PO Box 27779
San Diego, CA 92198
www.ReferencePointPress.com

LIBRARY OF CONGRESS CATALOGING-IN-PUBLICATION DATA

Name: Bode, Heather L., 1974– author.
Title: E-Sports and the World of Competitive Gaming/by Heather L. Bode.
Description: San Diego, CA: ReferencePoint Press, Inc., [2019] | Series: The World of Video Games | Audience: Grade 9 to 12 | Includes bibliographical references and index.
ISBN: 978-1-68282-557-0 (hardback)
ISBN: 978-1-68282-558-7 (ebook)
The complete Library of Congress record is available at www.loc.gov.

CONTENTS

IMPORTANT EVENTS IN THE HISTORY OF
VIDEO GAMES

1972
The Magnavox Odyssey, the first at-home gaming system, is introduced.

1969
Rick Blomme creates a two-person version of *Spacewar!* and releases it on PLATO.

1997
Dennis "Thresh" Fong wins a Ferrari 328 GTS as the grand prize of the first *Quake* tournament, Red Annihilation.

1965   **1975**   **1985**   **1995**   **2005**

1958
Physicist William Higinbotham creates the first video game, *Tennis for Two*.

1994
The ESRB is created to establish a ratings system for video games.

1980
Atari sponsors the first National *Space Invaders* Tournaments, drawing 10,000 participants.

2008
Four years after its release, *World of Warcraft* becomes the most popular massively multiplayer online (MMO) game with 11.5 million players.

4

2018
Epic's *Fortnite* Pro-Am becomes the first major *Fortnite: Battle Royale* tournament

2011
The popular E-Sports streaming service Twitch is launched.

2017
Team Liquid wins The International *Dota 2* tournament, becoming the first team to sweep the final round.

2018
The World Health Organization (WHO) adds gaming disorder to the 2018 International Classification of Diseases.

2015 **2016** **2017** **2018** **2019**

2015
Sixteen-year-old Sumail Hassan becomes the youngest E-Sports player to surpass $1,000,000 in earnings.

2017
The International Olympic Committee recognizes E-Sports as a sport and begins discussing the inclusion of E-Sports in the 2024 Olympics.

2018
E-Sports debuts at the Asian Games as a demonstration sport.

2017
PlayerUnknown's Battlegrounds is released, marking the beginning of battle royale games in E-Sports tournaments.

18th ASIAN GAMES

2018

ENERGY OF ASIA

GAMING AS A JOB

The crowd went wild in the arena. "It's done!" the commentator yelled. "[Team] Liquid will become the first team in the history of The International to whitewash the Grand Final, 3-0 victory!"[1] Confetti fluttered down around cheering fans. Onstage, competitors within a glass booth jumped from their computer chairs and hugged. As they exited the booth, camera crews moved in to capture the moment. Pyrotechnics erupted, lighting the path as Team Liquid walked up to claim the Aegis of Champions trophy.

In 2017, Team Liquid swept a final at The International, an E-Sports tournament for the game *Dota 2*. *Dota 2* is a free game in the multiplayer online battle arena (MOBA) genre, and it is the most played game on Steam, the world's most popular computer gaming platform. Team Liquid's winnings totaled almost $11 million of the $24 million prize pool. Such huge winnings make The International the largest E-Sports tournament in history. Team Liquid stated:

We have been dreaming of this moment since our first TI [The International] 4 years ago, and we can finally call ourselves International winners. With this victory, Team Liquid has now won the most prize money in the history of E-Sports.[2]

This is the world of E-Sports, where anyone can be a successful competitor not by sinking a basket or scoring a touchdown but by playing and showcasing the video games they love.

Many people gathered to watch The International, a Dota 2 tournament, in 2017. Team Liquid won prize money totaling $10.8 million at The International.

GOING MAINSTREAM

E-Sports is the latest in video game competition. It has become a phenomenon across the globe. The highest rated E-Sports tournaments feature teams that face off in arenas filled with loyal enthusiasts. The fans come dressed as their favorite E-Sports player or the player's onscreen avatar. Spectators watch the teams at their computers and follow the competition on huge screens throughout the arena. Just as in many traditional sports, commentators who are experts in a particular game describe the action and discuss strategies during matches.

With large numbers of players and fans having access to free video games such as *League of Legends* and *Dota 2,* E-Sports is becoming mainstream. The games grow in popularity as players compete with friends and fellow gamers. Statistics from SuperData, a video game market research company, show that as of 2017, "one in three people on the planet play free-to-play games across PC [personal computer] and mobile platforms."[3] According to a loyal E-Sports player, "It's a culture. There's just something about going online and finding three random people and playing a game with them that you all enjoy."[4] While the games inhabit imaginary worlds, the players are real.

For Sumail Hassan, known as SumaiL to his fans, his path to competitive E-Sports started in Pakistan at an age when most American kids are only in first or second grade. To play video games, Hassan sold his bike. Hassan and some of his family members would stack four people on his cousin's bike to travel to an internet café where they could play video games.

Hassan moved to the United States with his family when he was a teenager. His parents grew concerned about the amount of time he spent playing *Dota 2.* "No food, no water, only the computer for 18 hours," his father said.[5] The very reason Hassan was excited to come to the United States—greater internet access—was about to change his family forever. He was recruited by the E-Sports team Evil Geniuses. After only one month as a professional E-Sports player, Hassan had earned $200,000.

By 2015, at the age of 16, Hassan became the youngest E-Sports player to surpass $1,000,000 in earnings. This put him in the *Guinness Book of World Records*. The Evil Geniuses had just won the 2015

The International. Hassan said that "winning The International was all that mattered. I proved that I am the best."[6]

E-SPORTS TODAY

Debate remains as to whether E-Sports is truly a sport. There are many commonalities between traditional sports and E -Sports: trained players, rules and standards, coaches, teams, and leagues. There are amateurs, professionals, and solid fan bases. E-Sports players also have specialized equipment. Just as tennis players use particular rackets and basketball players use specialized shoes, E-Sports competitors have mice and keyboards designed for competition. But Team Liquid's Yiliang Peng, also known as Doublelift, doesn't think the debate is important. He says, "I don't care too much about the label. I'm a pro league player and I'm really proud of it."[7]

E-Sports, which originally gained popularity in South Korea and other Asian countries, has become a global force. It is now popular among younger generations in the United States, who are already familiar with video games and gaming culture. As E-Sports continues to evolve as an industry there remains much to learn. People are working to understand how these competitions will affect players, society, and the future of gaming.

> **"I don't care too much about the label. I'm a pro league player and I'm really proud of it."** [7]
>
> *–Yiliang Peng, Team Liquid member*

THE HISTORY OF
COMPETITIVE GAMING

Marketing research company Newzoo estimated that 380 million people would watch E-Sports in 2018. This makes E-Sports the fastest growing sport, both in viewers and players, on the planet. While baseball may be known as the United States' favorite pastime, E-Sports is quickly becoming people's favorite sport all over the world.

Many of today's video games are digital masterpieces that feature huge, meticulously crafted worlds, compelling storylines, and complex gameplay strategies. But sixty years ago, the first competitive video game had only a blip of light, two lines, and a joystick.

THE FIRST VIDEO GAME

In 1958, physicist William A. Higinbotham created what many people say is the first video game. Higinbotham prepared an interactive exhibit for the annual Visitors' Day at Brookhaven National Laboratory in New York. He worked there as the head of the Instrumentation Division. The game weighed 300 pounds (136 kg) and was a maze of circuitry connected to an oscilloscope, a machine used to display electronic waves. The two-person tennis simulation, based on Higinbotham's work calculating ballistic missile trajectories, was called *Tennis for Two.* Higinbotham never filed for a patent. *Tennis for Two*

E-Sports tournaments happen in countries all over the world. In 2017 there was a Counter-Strike: Global Offensive *tournament in Saint Petersburg, Russia.*

was the first of many similar tennis and ping-pong games that would arrive on the market in the early years of video gaming. According to a pamphlet published by the Instrumentation Division, "By all accounts, the game was a huge success. Willy Higinbotham was amazed that people were lined up completely around the gym to wait their turn to play."[8] People were very interested in digital competitive games.

But Ralph Baer, not Higinbotham, became known as the father of E-Sports. Baer was a World War II (1939–1945) veteran who earned a degree in television engineering. Baer pioneered the concept of using an ordinary TV to display a game in which two players could compete against each other. Baer said, "We built a succession of seven models, the last one of which we called the Brown Box. . . .

At-home gaming was first introduced in the 1970s. Today, millions of people play video games at home.

then we went on a two-year trek trying to find somebody who would take a license and actually produce something. That turned out to be Magnavox."[9] Known as the Magnavox Odyssey, Baer's invention was the first at-home video game console, released in 1972. It also came with two controllers and the first video game gun accessory. Between 1972 and 1975, Magnavox produced and sold 700,000 Odysseys. The home video game industry had begun.

NETWORKED GAMES

Computers were originally invented for business and scientific use, but they soon began appearing on college campuses. In 1960, professor Don Bitzer developed the Programmed Logic for Automatic Teaching Operations (PLATO) system at the University of Illinois, Urbana.

PLATO started out as an educational platform just for students at the University of Illinois, but as more people began using it, PLATO became a global interpersonal communication system. It set the precedent for the World Wide Web and the internet.

In 1969, a member of the PLATO staff named Rick Blomme altered a single-player game called *Spacewar!* to a two-player version which could be accessed remotely via PLATO. This was the beginning of networked multiplayer games. By 1979, PLATO was available all over the world. There were all-nighters for playing online games, split screen chats, email, and even emoticons. Many early video game designers were influenced by PLATO.

MULTI-USER DUNGEONS

Multi-user dungeons (MUDs) were early text-based, role-playing video games. They were based on earlier tabletop role-playing games such as *Dungeons & Dragons*. These tabletop games helped pave the way for more complex and competitive video games. Ethan Gilsdorf, an avid *Dungeons & Dragons* player in his youth, says, "The game taught the concept of role-playing to millions. It was a groundbreaking step for immersive escapism entertainment."[10]

MUDs required the use of a player's imagination to navigate characters through fantasy settings and obstacles. While in a MUD, players read descriptions of their fantastical avatars, the environment, and fellow players. They made their way through a world without graphics, interacting and communicating through short commands typed into the computer.

Speaking of the legacy of these games, Gilsdorf says, "Online games, especially Massively Multi-Player Online Role-Playing Games [MMORPGs], tend to focus on longer narratives, quests, and relationships that can last for months or years. Thousands of players inhabit a 'persistent' game world."[11] *World of Warcraft,* a popular MMORPG introduced in 2004, uses the concepts of dungeons and raids that were developed in the first MUDs.

> **"Online games . . . tend to focus on longer narratives, quests, and relationships that can last for months or years. Thousands of players inhabit a 'persistent' game world."** [11]
>
> –*Ethan Gilsdorf, author of* Fantasy Freaks and Gaming Geeks

THE ARCADE ERA

Most video game experts agree that the genre of E-Sports began with arcades, places where people went to play the latest games. They gained popularity in the 1970s and 1980s. Video game cabinets for games such as *Pac-Man* and *Donkey Kong* were expensive, costing upwards of $1,700. But arcades were accessible to people of all generations. With a good supply of quarters, gamers enjoyed hours of entertainment. It created a feeling of community as well as competition. According to an arcade enthusiast: "A sense of community existed in every video game arcade. Our successes and failures were both public and short lived. . . . Back then, it also became a social ritual in which we made new friends based on a shared interest in mastering a series of electronic puzzles."[12]

One of the developments of arcade games was the concept of the high score list. Many video games displayed gamers' initials in a list of

DONKEY KONG

In 2007, the documentary *The King of Kong* followed two players vying for the highest score on the 1981 arcade game *Donkey Kong*. Billy Mitchell and Steve Wiebe garnered their own followings as people either sided with the underdog, Wiebe, or the reigning champion, Mitchell. Mitchell won with a score of 1,047,200, becoming the first person to achieve a score over 1 million. But in 2018, Mitchell was stripped of his title. He was caught cheating at *Donkey Kong*, using a modified version of the game to get his high scores. Wiebe finally received recognition for being the first person to score over 1 million points. By February 2018, the highest score honor belonged to Robbie Lakeman, who broke the record with 1,247,700.

the top-scoring players. This added competition as well as a desire to come back and maintain one's high score.

Arcade games made a global impact unforeseen by their creators. One such game was *Space Invaders*, made in 1978 by Japanese game developer Tomohiro Nishikado. The goal of the game was to defend a space station from alien attacks. The player controlled a laser cannon with which the aliens had to be blasted before reaching Earth.

Japan eventually had 100,000 *Space Invaders* arcade cabinets throughout the country. Steven Kent, a video game historian, says, "So many people were playing the game that it caused a national coin shortage. The Japanese mint had to triple the production of the 100-yen piece because so many coins were glutted in the arcades."[13]

By 1980, the game had become popular in the United States. Game company Atari sponsored the first National Space Invaders Tournament. It drew 10,000 participants. Regional tournaments were held all over the United States, and news coverage ensured video game enthusiasts were aware of the tournament. Gamers became

Space Invaders *was a popular arcade game in the 1970s. An at-home version was released in 1980 for the Atari 2600.*

fascinated with the idea of competitive gaming on a much larger scale than the local arcade.

MS. PAC-MAN AND MODDING

Although space-themed games were extremely popular, it was *Ms. Pac-Man* that was destined to become the highest-selling arcade game. The original *Pac-Man* was invented by Toru Iwatani in 1979. Iwatani wanted to create a nonviolent game with hopes of appealing to a larger consumer base. His game design was based on eating. "The actual figure of *Pac-Man* came about as I was having pizza for lunch. I took one wedge and there it was, the figure of *Pac-Man,"* said Iwatani.[14]

The entire video game industry changed with the release of *Pac-Man.* Maze games appeared in a variety of forms. A cartoon was developed based on the *Pac-Man* character, and a song entitled "Pac-Man Fever" sold over one million copies.

Iwatani was not involved with the creation of *Ms. Pac-Man.* It was an early example of what is today known as modding. Nine college students created enhancement kits that were manufactured and placed onto the circuit boards of existing games. Once the kit was in place, the game worked differently—it had been modded, or modified. Ms. Pac-Man had a bow on top of her circular shape and wore lipstick. In addition to Ms. Pac-Man's changed appearance,

> **"The actual figure of *Pac-Man* came about as I was having pizza for lunch. I took one wedge and there it was, the figure of *Pac-Man.***" [14]
>
> *–Toru Iwatani, inventor of* Pac-Man

there were new mazes, characters, and cutscenes in the game. Atari originally took the college students to court. But the two sides reached an agreement under which Atari continued manufacturing the *Pac-Man* circuitry and the students produced the enhancement kits. *Ms. Pac-Man,* under the Atari name, became the biggest selling arcade game in the United States, with 115,000 units sold.

BULLETIN BOARD SYSTEMS AND LOCAL AREA NETWORKS

Avid online gamers were ready to pay for opportunities to compete with like-minded gamers over the internet. In the 1970s, they began using early online communication tools called Bulletin Board Systems (BBS) to connect with other players. For the cost of a phone call, users connected and logged in using a modem over a phone line. Then, using a text-based BBS, they posted information including gameplay tips and strategies or invites to play games. Since long distance calls were more expensive, the BBS tended to be local, making it easier for those with common interests to meet face to face and hold gatherings.

Another way gamers met was through local area network (LAN) parties. At a LAN party, people arrived at a designated location with their desktop computers for multiplayer gaming. They would use networking cables to physically connect their computers, forming a LAN. Although it was awkward to haul the large equipment, gamers stayed for hours or days participating in face-to-face competition. In these ways, gaming communities were formed.

FIGHTING GAMES AND *STREET FIGHTER II*

Two-player fighting games entered the arcades in the late 1970s with games like *Heavyweight Champ* and *Warrior.* Graphics were crude, and gameplay was sluggish by today's standards. By the time *Street Fighter II* was released in 1991, the advances in technology were evident. As one historian says, "*Street Fighter II* introduced the smoothest animation and the fastest, most complex controls ever seen, and when it came out, the arcades suddenly breathed new life, and one-on-one fighters rapidly became the new 'killer app.'"[15]

Each fighter had his or her own signature moves, strengths, and weaknesses. Like real martial arts, the game required practice and mastery. Tim Skelly, the game designer of *Warrior,* says that similarly to rumors surrounding *Space Invaders'* popularity in Japan, "*Street Fighter II* would become so popular that rumors circulated claiming that the game was causing coin shortages."[16]

Fighting games, including *Street Fighter II* and its sequels, would become a staple of the E-Sports scene. The highest-profile fighting game event in the world is the Evolution Championship Series—better known simply as Evo. The top players in the world compete in several of the most popular fighting games in front of cheering crowds of devoted fans. The 2018 event featured such games as *Street Fighter V, Super Smash Bros. Melee*, and *Tekken 7.* Winners took home thousands of dollars in cash prizes.

> **"*Street Fighter II* would become so popular that rumors circulated claiming that the game was causing coin shortages." [16]**
>
> *–Tim Skelly, game designer*

FIRST-PERSON SHOOTERS

Doom was released in 1993 by id Software. It was a revolutionary first-person shooter (FPS) game that launched a gaming community. *Doom* wasn't the first FPS, but its superior design, faster gameplay, and immersive music set it apart from its competitors. Another unique aspect of *Doom* was the way that id distributed the game. The company allowed the introductory levels to be given away freely as shareware. This meant people were encouraged to make and share copies of these portions of the game. If people enjoyed the game, they could purchase the full version. *Doom* also popularized the concept of the death match mode. In this mode, players hunted each other instead of computer-controlled monsters. The goal was to kill or "frag" as many players as possible within a certain time limit.

Quake, released in 1996, represented another leap forward in the FPS genre. *Quake* improved on *Doom*'s technology with the introduction of stunning, fully three-dimensional graphics and more multiplayer options. The makers of both *Doom* and *Quake* encouraged modding by releasing the source code for their games. Whereas with *Ms. Pac-Man*, college students had to work backwards to discover the game's code, id Software simply published theirs. This has helped the games remain popular for decades.

From *Ms. Pac-Man* to *Quake*, gaming companies realized the importance of giving gamers the ability to mod games. Many of the current top E-Sports games are mods of predecessors. *Defense of the Ancients (Dota)* was a mod of the game *Warcraft III*. The game developer Valve purchased the intellectual property of *Dota* and released *Dota 2* in 2013. The FPS *Counter-Strike* was modded from an earlier Valve game called *Half-Life*. Its sequel, *Counter-Strike: Global Offensive (CS:GO)* is a popular E-Sports game.

In 1997 id Software held Red Annihilation, the first *Quake* tournament. Red Annihilation became legendary because of its grand prize, a Ferrari 328 GTS belonging to *Quake* cocreator John Carmack. Red Annihilation provided a national stage for online gaming and made an already well-known player famous. Dennis "Thresh" Fong was undefeated in practice matches and competitive play. He had popularized the technique of rocket-jumping, propelling his avatar into the air by firing his weapon at the ground. Fong soundly

CS:GO *remains a popular E-Sports title for tournaments. It is played at the* DreamHack Masters *tournament in Malmo, Sweden.*

beat his opponent. While some people believe that Fong's win at Red Annihilation started the interest in E-Sports, Fong attributes it to the quality of *Quake*'s game design. Fong is regarded as the first professional gamer. The character "Thresh" in *League of Legends* was named after him. In 2016, Fong was inducted into the E-Sports Hall of Fame.

MMORPG COMMUNITIES

The first MMORPG available to the public was *Meridian 59.* It was released in 1996. Players roamed pixelated streets of a fantasy city called Barloque. As battles and rivalries commenced, friendships also formed. Some people who began playing in the 1990s as teenagers still play the game in 2018.

The first commercially successful MMORPG was *Ultima Online*, released in 1997. *Ultima Online* not only had cutting-edge graphics but also supported thousands of players on multiple servers. *Ultima Online* continues to add expansion packs featuring new content to keep challenging players more than two decades after its initial release.

REAL-TIME STRATEGY

In real-time strategy (RTS) games, combat and economics are both important. Winning depends on resource management, strategy, and careful timing. Players typically view the action from a birds-eye view, directing the action of their fighters and resource-gatherers below. The best-selling game of 1998 was Blizzard Entertainment's RTS game *StarCraft*. In *StarCraft*, gamers choose one of three species fighting for galactic dominance. Game developer Bob Fitch spent fifty to eighty hours per week developing *StarCraft*. At that time, he said, "If I want to play the game when I am sleeping here, showering here, and people are bringing me my food—then this game is going to be great."[17] *StarCraft* became a global phenomenon, gaining particular popularity in South Korea. Hui "Moffy" Kyung says, "The reason *StarCraft* was so popular in Korea was not only because it was such a well-made game, it was because it played a major role in leading the culture at that time."[18] Mike Morhaime, cofounder of Blizzard, visited South Korea and observed his first *StarCraft* E-Sports tournament. He said, "It was incredible. The crowd was really into it and they were cheering every time something happened. It was so much fun and there were so many people there. The fans were completely into it.

It was amazing."[19] Morhaime returned to the United States inspired to start similar tournaments.

Blizzard Entertainment and Valve, together with *League of Legends* creators Riot Games, are some of the largest gaming companies in the US E-Sports landscape. The games they produce, along with those of their competitors, have made gaming the most popular form of entertainment in the world, worth almost three times as much as the movie industry.

> "It was incredible. The crowd was really into it and they were cheering every time something happened. It was so much fun and there were so many people there." [19]
>
> –Mike Morhaime, cofounder of Blizzard

HOW DO PEOPLE
PLAY E-SPORTS?

"The notion of converting something you love into something you can do as a vocation holds an almost mythical status in our culture, a goal only the luckiest few attain," says T.L. Taylor, a video game researcher.[20] The path to becoming a professional gamer can be daunting. But the high number of people participating in E-Sports, combined with the visibility of gameplay through streaming, means that video game hobbyists can entertain the possibility of transforming a leisure activity into a paying job.

AMATEUR PLAYERS

With the proliferation of games available on mobile devices, consoles, and computers, there are a variety of ways to play video games. Almost all of these ways can be done alone within the confines of a home. But with E-Sports, the multiplayer aspect is key. When players are able to easily beat a game's computer-controlled opponents, they seek out greater challengers and often begin playing within a circle of friends. When this loses novelty and a player still has the drive to master the game, they look for other outlets of play. This extends the social circle beyond face-to-face competitions and into the wider gaming community. Taylor notes, "Many average and casual players

GETTING A WINNING EDGE

Ping time is crucial to online gamers. This refers to the amount of time it takes for gaming computers to communicate with the game server. Researcher T.L. Taylor says, "If one of you has a poorer connection (higher ping time) it is going to show through lag in executed moves, what you see on the screen, your feel for the action, and your general ability to act and react." As a result, having a high-quality internet connection is important to competitive online gamers—especially when the games they play require lightning-fast reaction times.

Players can also gain a competitive edge through the peripherals they use. Peripherals are computer accessories such as mice and keyboards. Players often bring their own preferred peripherals to tournaments. Taylor continues:

> When competitors sit down and set up, you often see them quickly move their mouse back and forth across the mouse pad to get a feel for it, to reconnect the embodied action interfacing with peripheral to the digital space.

Peripherals play such a large role that some websites list players' specific devices. Top players may even endorse particular models, earning an extra stream of income from the peripheral company.

T.L. Taylor, Raising the Stakes: E-Sports and the Professionalization of Computer Gaming. *Cambridge, MA: MIT Press, 2015, p. 41.*

will never hit the online functionality of a game and seek out new people to compete against."[21] However, gamers who are serious about playing professionally will quickly seek out the most challenging opponents they can find.

Some competitive games can be played by a solo gamer, but others require assembling a team. In these games, it can be difficult for an isolated player to form new team connections. The focus of amateur online leagues is to aid gamers who want to test new strategies and form bonds with like-minded players. One league

> **"There are more than 150 million gamers in the United States alone—there's no reason only a few top players should enjoy everything gaming competition has to offer."** [22]
>
> *–Ethos, E-Sports league organization*

organization, Ethos, states: "There are more than 150 million gamers in the United States alone—there's no reason only a few top players should enjoy everything gaming competition has to offer."[22]

Amateur online leagues use a variety of methods including skill level and style of play to match gamers with comparable opponents or possible teammates. Gamers pay a membership fee. Through successful match play, gamers earn points and begin playing tougher opponents. Some games, such as Blizzard's FPS *Overwatch,* have their own dedicated websites to promote amateur play. Other websites offer similar services for a wide variety of games across multiple genres. As E-Sports continues its expansion across the globe, new organizations will surface to support competitive gaming at the amateur level. Building up a strong base of amateur players will help train the next generation of professional E-Sports gamers.

PROFESSIONAL GAMERS

Professional gamers tend to focus on a single game. They are also highly competitive. But making the adjustment from playing at home, in anonymity with an online community, to playing on a live E-Sports stage is stark. The center stage features face-to-face competition.

Spotlights flash, commentators analyze each mouse click, referees look over shoulders, and the travel, intensity, and high stakes can wear on the nerves of players.

Professionals have both an expertise in their game and an understanding of ways to get a competitive edge. They know the game's shortcuts, places where they might encounter glitches, and the capabilities of characters, weapons, and items. They may also study the specific strengths and weaknesses of the gamers they play against. Professionals must have a high level of tactical and strategic thinking, along with sharp reaction times. What looks like mere button-pushing can win a game. "At the core, skilled computer game players are engaging in a kind of familiar complex strategic and tactical mastery, a sophisticated form of cognitive and physical work, mediated through technology and perfected through hours of play with others," says Taylor.[23]

Clinton "Fear" Loomis was already a *Dota 2* legend when he was featured in Valve's 2014 YouTube documentary *Free to Play*. Loomis told his mother he wanted to be a professional gamer before *Dota 2* even existed. He said, "I'm a very competitive person. Gaming fulfills my

> **"At the core, skilled computer game players are engaging in a kind of familiar complex strategic and tactical mastery, a sophisticated form of cognitive and physical work, mediated through technology and perfected through hours of play with others."** [23]
>
> *–T.L. Taylor, video game researcher*

competitive need."[24] Known as a calm, father-type figure, Loomis has mentored younger players for years. In 2018, at the age of thirty, Loomis was released by Evil Geniuses, the US team he had captained as a player and coached when injured. "Don't worry guys," Loomis tweeted, "Happy I get some time at home after a very exhausting and disappointing season. Wish everyone all the best."[25]

AGE AND INJURIES

In 2017, ESPN researched the average age of professional athletes in various sports. The results read:

> *E-Sports players are significantly younger than their counterparts in other major sports. The average age of the opening day rosters in the most recent season at the highest professional level in football, basketball, baseball and hockey was higher than the average age of any of the E-Sports games we analyzed.[26]*

For example, the average *League of Legends* player was 21.2 years old, while the average NFL player was 26.6 years old. Some gamers believe a slowing reaction time plays a role in this. In 2014, the manager of the E-Sports team Na'Vi said, "Regarding age, 25 or 26 is the absolute maximum. Your reaction time lowers after that. You can't click so much as the kids do."[27] Along with this comes physical injury. The main causes of injury to E-Sports players are carpal tunnel syndrome, tennis elbow, and trigger finger. Carpal tunnel syndrome occurs when a nerve running from the forearm to the palm of the hand gets compressed. It causes pain, numbness, and weakness. Tennis elbow is an overuse injury due to repetitive motion. It occurs where the forearm muscles attach to the elbow. Pain can radiate down the arm to the hand. Trigger finger occurs when a finger gets stuck in a

The team Evil Genuises has members who play many different types of games. Professional E-Sports players typically only play one game for their team.

bent position. Anyone working in an occupation involving the gripping motion, such as a mouse, is at a higher risk for trigger finger.

Any of these conditions can derail a gamer, as they are all arm-related injuries. Rest is needed for recovery, and in severe cases surgery may be needed. Stretching and performing particular exercises prior to gaming can reduce the risk of injury.

THE GAMES

A handful of games dominate the E-Sports landscape. Several of them—including *League of Legends* and *Dota 2*—are in the MOBA genre. *League of Legends* was released by Riot Games in 2009. Combining real-time strategy with role-playing, gamers choose a champion character to battle opponents. The goal is to destroy the enemy Nexus while protecting your own Nexus. A top-down perspective is utilized, which allows gamers to see a map-like terrain as they plot their course. By 2018, Newzoo reported that *League of Legends* topped the charts on Twitch, a service through which users can watch people streaming and playing video games. That same year, people spent 274.7 million hours watching *League of Legends* at E-Sports competitions and 742.5 million hours watching *League of Legends* outside of formal competitions. Newzoo says these numbers are not surprising, "as it is the biggest E-Sports title in the world with many popular streamers."[28]

Dota 2, released by Valve in 2013, is the top E-Sports game in terms of prize money. In the game, two opposing teams choose heroes to battle the enemy. Routes known as lanes connect the player's base to the enemy's base, and these lanes become the focus of the battle. Players try to reach the enemy's base and destroy a structure called the Ancient. *Dota 2*'s main tournament, The International, accumulates large prize pools by crowdfunding.

World of Warcraft, released in 2004, is an MMORPG set in the universe of Blizzard's Warcraft RTS games. Heroes complete quests using magical weapons and spells. Much of the game is played cooperatively, with players teaming up to fight computer-controlled enemies. But in areas called Arenas, players can instead battle each other. The Arena World Championship is the *World of Warcraft* E-Sports competition. It culminates with the top 12 teams facing off at BlizzCon, the annual gaming convention hosted by Blizzard.

Heroes of the Storm is another popular title by Blizzard. Released in 2015, this MOBA features well-known heroes and villains from Blizzard's other famed game series, including Warcraft, Diablo, and StarCraft. Players choose a faction to play for and a hero to control.

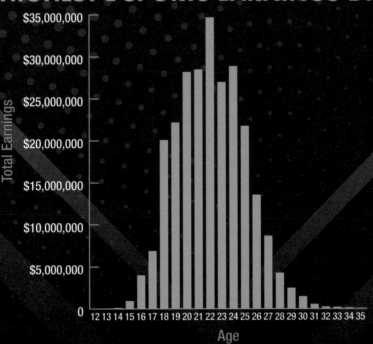

As of September 2018, E-Sports gamers who were twenty-two years old had earned the highest earnings by age at over $34.7 million. They were also one of the largest groups, totaling 1,440 players. The largest group of players was twenty-year-olds, which totaled 1,641 players. However, the number of players per year after that drops dramatically. For example, there were only 765 twenty-five-year-olds and only 12 thirty-five-year-olds. Additionally, the group of 35-year-olds only made $93,700 in earnings in 2018.

According to Dr. John T. Holden of Florida State University, "It is not uncommon for E-Sports professionals to retire from competition at an age of 19, occasionally choosing to pursue a career streaming or coaching." Holden believes that one reason for the drop-off in both earnings and number of players is that "professional and amateur video-gaming is physical and mental exhaustion."

John T. Holden, "Esports: Children, Stimulants, and Video Gaming-induced Inactivity," Journal of Pediatrics and Child Health, February 20, 2018. www.ncbi.nlm.nih.gov

SPEEDRUNNING

Not all competitive games involve two players battling head-to-head at the same time. Speedrunning is another popular form of competitive gaming. This is completing a game in the fastest time possible. Speedrunners adhere to guidelines which vary from game to game. Multiple types of speedruns are available. Speedruns can be completed with or without taking advantage of glitches in the game's programming. Speedrunning at 100% means all the game's secrets and items must be found during the speedrun, while Any% speedrunning allows players to skip these requirements and simply find the fastest path to the ending. After accumulated hours of play, speedrunners gain an intimate knowledge of the intricate details of how games work. Speedrunning has a large fan community, and many enthusiasts enjoy watching live streams of speedrunners to help improve their own skill and understanding of a game.

Each battle arena map comes with its own set of challenges and objectives. *Heroes of the Storm* requires practice and methodical patience to determine how each hero benefits the team in a new setting. Leveling up is very important as it unlocks new abilities for the heroes, and as with all MOBAs, teammate communication is key to success. *Heroes of the Storm* has become so popular that it spawned a college-aged competition called Heroes of the Dorm.

Several of the top E-Sports games are FPSs. Blizzard's *Overwatch*, released in 2016, quickly became a hit. Teams of six heroes battle on a variety of diverse maps. Each hero must choose a team role. Some are on offense, moving quickly and dealing damage to the enemy. Others are in a tank role, absorbing enemy fire and drawing the opponents away from the rest of the team. Players must learn how their hero's skills can benefit the team. *Overwatch* has become so popular, it has its own franchised league, *Overwatch League*, with teams representing major cities such as Seoul, South Korea, and Philadelphia, Pennsylvania. The *Overwatch* World Cup is an annual competition culminating in the best teams competing at BlizzCon.

CS:GO is an FPS released by Valve in 2012. Second only to *League of Legends* in number of hours spent watching it as an E-Sport, *CS:GO* is a fast-paced, skill-based game. Two teams face off as either terrorists or counter-terrorists. They encounter secondary objectives along the way, such as hostage rescues. Death is permanent in *CS:GO*—until the next game starts. Players do not level up or gain new skills or items as they play, meaning that all players are on an even playing field. Still, regular players have an advantage over newer players thanks to their intimate knowledge of the maps and their carefully honed reaction times.

PlayerUnknown's Battlegrounds, commonly known as *PUBG* for short, is an online multiplayer battle royale video game. This genre burst onto the scene in 2017, and it quickly became wildly popular. In battle royale games, a large number of players compete in a single match, killing each other to become the last person standing. In *PUBG*, 100 players parachute onto a huge island where they must collect weapons and supplies to ensure their survival. As players are eliminated, the map area shrinks, forcing players to encounter each other more frequently. According to SuperData, "*PlayerUnknown's Battlegrounds* was 2017's breakout success, generating $712 million in revenue in just eight months."[29] It was also the "most watched new title on Twitch," according to Newzoo.[30]

Because of *PUBG*'s success, a similar battle royale game called *Fortnite: Battle Royale* emerged. Released by Epic Games in 2017,

Fortnite: Battle Royale resembles *PUBG* in many ways. The game begins with 100 players parachuting onto an island, and the last one alive is the winner. While both games are battle royales, *PUBG* feels more serious, grounded, and realistic. *Fortnite* is more colorful and lighthearted. In *Fortnite,* a gamer explains, "Your character doesn't technically die. A little drone comes and picks you up. It's more cartoony."[31] *Fortnite* is also set apart by its focus on building structures. Players can build defensive walls or forts in the middle of a match, adding a new layer of strategy to the genre.

> **"Your character doesn't technically die. A little drone comes and picks you up. It's more cartoony."** [31]
>
> *–anonymous* Fortnite *player*

In June 2018, the first major *Fortnite: Battle Royale* tournament was held in Los Angeles, California. Epic's *Fortnite* Pro-Am was peppered with famous *Fortnite* streamers including Tyler "Ninja" Blevins and Ali "Myth" Kabbani, along with a variety of sports and TV celebrities. Kabbani, who was 19 at the time of the Pro-Am, takes his prominence seriously, explaining, "When it comes to me being a hero for these kids, I just want to promote the best message I can. I don't want them to idolize me, but just use me as a center of influence. That's something I think about a lot."[32]

TRAINING FACILITIES

The evolution of E-Sports continues through the development of professional training facilities. Before, some teams were composed of isolated players who only met in person for tournament play.

Other teams held training sessions at team houses. In team houses, teams live together but the setting is casual, and there is little direct contact with the team's management. The latest E-Sports facilities have more in common with the elite training facilities of traditional professional sports teams.

Team Liquid, based in Los Angeles, has one such facility. It features a dining area, conference rooms, an area to review game footage, and a production studio for creating web content. One reporter notes that this E-Sports facility aims to:

> not only improve the caliber of current players and develop prospects into future pros, but also instill a culture of professionalism to a group of players used to operating on their own from remote locations or in team houses in which players both work and reside.[33]

Those involved with the development of this E-Sports training facility concept are working with an already proven system in place within other professional sports. Team Liquid, one of the most well-known E-Sports teams, has a roster of more than fifty professional gamers. The team's financial backers reflect an impressive list of investors who also own or co-own teams such as the NBA's Golden State Warriors and Washington Wizards, MLB's Los Angeles Dodgers, MLS's Los Angeles Football Club, and the NHL's Washington Capitals. As one co-owner says, "We wanted to make sure that we had a culture from day one that treated E-Sports players as professionals."[34]

LEAGUES, TOURNAMENTS, AND EVENTS

Over the years, different professional E-Sports leagues have been established and discontinued. Some of the current leagues include the Electronic Sports League (ESL), Major League Gaming (MLG), and ELEAGUE. The ESL has built a fan base by offering different games that are popular in each region. It also encourages beginner and amateur players as well as its elite players. MLG focuses on console games in addition to some computer games. Streaming and video on demand have helped to build its fan base. ELEAGUE features live broadcasts on Twitch and the television network TBS. Partnering with the computer company Dell, it intends to attract audiences with the use of cutting-edge technology for its gamers.

Major E-Sports events typically feature commentators and referees. The earliest E-Sports commentators were often former players who used the knowledge they had to stay connected to their favorite games. Today's commentators view multiple screens from a variety of perspectives to act as storytellers, not only communicating what is happening in the game, but also offering statistics, player profiles, and history to viewers. Due to a lack of standardized records in E-Sports history, some commentators keep their own statistics. When a tournament or league no longer exists, the accompanying websites may be shut down, and parts of E-Sports history are lost. Commentators often play the games themselves to better understand what unfolds during a match, and there is a lot of studying to learn terms specific to a game. One commentator says, "It has its own little language and it's important you recognize that and use it appropriately when you commentate. Otherwise you'd look like an idiot."[35] It is also becoming more common to analyze statistics on different games and E-Sports players.

E-Sports referees make sure gaming tournaments stay fair and competitive. The refs can not only hear what all the gamers are saying but can also talk to any of the players at any time. E-Sports refs must search for glitches and cheating, and they ensure transitions between games go smoothly. They also share a passion for E-Sports. Raven Keene, the former head referee for the North American League Championship Series, says, "I'm a fan to the core. You get to see a completely different perspective being behind the players. It's invigorating."[36]

Blizzard Entertainment's BlizzCon marked its twelfth year in 2018. Featuring contests for costumes and art, as well as charity auctions, BlizzCon is the home of the *Heroes of the Storm* Global Championship, the *Overwatch* World Cup, the *StarCraft* World Championship Series and more.

Valve's tournament, The International, is the pinnacle of *Dota 2*'s pro circuit. The tournament is known for its large prize pool, historically the largest in E-Sports, which increases every time a gamer purchases a Battle Pass. When ordinary players buy a Battle Pass, they get the chance to obtain exclusive features and rewards in *Dota 2*. A portion of the cost of the Battle Pass goes directly into The International's prize pool. Valve offers incentives, and displays the running total of the prize pool on *Dota 2's* website to keep gamers informed.

Riot Games features the *League of Legends* League Championship Series (LCS), which

> **"I'm a fan to the core. You get to see a completely different perspective being behind the players. It's invigorating."** [36]
>
> *–Raven Keene, former head referee for the North American League Championship Series*

BlizzCon is a yearly event hosted by Blizzard Entertainment. The company created World of Warcraft *and other popular games.*

is divided into major global divisions: the North American (NA) LCS, the European (EU) LCS, and the *League of Legends* Champions Korea (LCK). Qualifying rounds begin in September and the finals are in November. The LCS also hosts the Mid-Season Invitational tournament. In 2018, the final match of the Mid-Season Invitational had 60 million viewers.

E-SPORTS AND IMMIGRATION

Many E-Sports teams travel the world to participate in tournaments. Within a team, several nationalities may be represented. International players traveling to the United States to play E-Sports have faced some challenges with US immigration policies, and some policies have even changed to accommodate them.

E-Sports teams have regular seasons, called splits. And just like traditional sports teams, during splits, players often can be traded or choose to move to a different team. But this may also mean a continental move, such as from Europe to the United States. Working and receiving pay in a country where you do not have citizenship is strictly regulated.

Non-US players need to obtain a non-immigrant visa if they intend to stay and work within the United States. Visas have many classifications, and without the proper documentation, players face legal ramifications affecting their jobs and those of their teammates. To help this process, Riot Games, the company behind *League of Legends,* petitioned the United States Immigration and Citizenship Services. They asked that E-Sports players be recognized as athletes. This allows them to apply for a P-1A visa for artists, entertainers, and athletes. While Riot's petition was successful, E-Sports players must still go through many steps providing documentation, including proving that they are internationally recognized, before being granted this type of visa. Many continue to be denied. As the proliferation of E-Sports gathers momentum and gains recognition, immigration policies around the world may change to better recognize E-Sports and individuals pursuing careers in professional gaming.

CHAPTER 3

HOW DO Ɛ-SPORTS
AFFECT SOCIETY?

As a global phenomenon, both on the amateur and professional level, E-Sports and competitive gaming are having considerable impacts on society. As with any phenomenon, there are both positive and negative effects to evaluate.

STREAMING

The popularity of competitive gaming is closely tied to the rise of widespread high-speed internet access. Being able to view live streams and videos showing skilled professional gamers playing video games has changed the landscape of competitive gaming. Viewers can watch not just as fans, but also as dedicated gamers themselves, picking up techniques they can apply to their own gameplay. Streamers can become celebrities, gaining fans due to their personalities and for their funny banter during matches.

The two largest platforms streaming E-Sports are Twitch and YouTube. SuperData reports, "97% of U.S. E-Sports viewers choose to watch competitions on either Twitch or YouTube."[37] Twitch emerged as a games-focused service as the concept of game streaming began to take off. YouTube shows all kinds of videos, but its YouTube Gaming division has grown to become a major player in the game streaming industry. Through both platforms, prominent players are able to create their own bands of loyal followers. Both platforms are now owned by business powerhouses. Twitch was purchased by Amazon for $970 million in 2014, while YouTube was purchased by Google in 2006 for $1.6 billion. YouTube and Twitch both depend on advertisers for revenue. Individual streamers earn income through viewer subscriptions.

Each platform has its own strengths, weaknesses, and devoted users. YouTube fans like the consistency of one-stop viewing: all kinds of videos, gaming or otherwise, can be viewed on the same site. YouTube also provides extremely sharp video quality. Another favorite YouTube Gaming feature is the ability to pause during a live stream.

Twitch is known for enhanced chatting capabilities. It was the lone dominant player in streaming before YouTube Gaming premiered, and it continues to hold a strong following. In 2017, Twitch hosted 54 percent of all gaming video content—with YouTube and all other smaller and similar streaming companies holding the remaining 46 percent. These streaming platforms have created a new career field for avid gamers.

Tyler "Ninja" Blevins makes his living as a full-time streamer. But when he started streaming, he was also going to college, holding down a job, and competing in tournaments for *Halo*, a popular FPS franchise. When he began streaming *Fortnite: Battle Royale*, his following showed explosive growth. In January 2018, Blevins had just under 900,000 followers. By June, that number was over 8 million, making him Twitch's top streamer of 2018. Blevins believes he can pinpoint the reason for his success:

> *I offer a combination of high tier gameplay that they [viewers] can't get with a lot of other content creators. It's difficult to be one of the best at any video game or anything else in the world. I'm very goofy. If you've ever watched my streams or YouTube videos, I do impressions and crazy shenanigans. It's the combination of that. It's a hybrid.*[38]

With 8 million followers on Twitch along with additional followers on YouTube Gaming, Blevins's income reached an estimated $500,000 per month in 2018. The success of Twitch, YouTube Gaming, and individual celebrity streamers demonstrates how competitive gaming has helped to drive a whole new online industry.

> "It's difficult to be one of the best at any video game or anything else in the world. I'm very goofy. If you've ever watched my streams or YouTube videos, I do impressions and crazy shenanigans."[38]
>
> –Tyler Blevins, video game streamer

SPONSORSHIPS AND FRANCHISES

"In 2017, the implementation of the franchising system in the E-Sports industry kicked off," reported Newzoo.[39] Within the league structure, franchising means teams no longer need to worry about being dropped from a league or struggling to remain in one. If a team buys a franchise slot in a league, that team is guaranteed a permanent spot in that league. In some cases, this gives the team a home tied to a geographic location. Fans will benefit from not losing a favorite team, broadcasters can be hired for repeated services, and obtaining team sponsors can become less complicated. The *Overwatch* League is an example of this newer franchise system.

Sponsorships are vital to the E-Sports industry and economy. Teams walking to center stage at major events are typically wearing jackets or jerseys touting sponsorships. Without sponsors, prize money could dry up and tournaments could shut down. Professionals would not have funding to pursue gaming as an occupation, and the E-Sports industry could shrink considerably.

Gaining and maintaining sponsorships requires a combination of trust and commitment by all involved parties. A sponsor provides monetary support and sometimes merchandise. In return, the sponsor receives product and brand promotion along with increased visibility. In 2015, it was estimated that the value of the traditional sports sponsorship market was $50 billion per year. One student researcher said, "When adding the high visibility and extensive coverage by both written press and media, the whole world is within reach when sponsoring popular sports events such as the FIFA World Cup or the Olympics."[40] The audience for E-Sports has begun to approach that global scale. Sponsors and teams evaluate whether they are both benefitting from the relationship. If a team player displays poor behavior on social media, this not only impacts the player's reputation, but also that of the sponsor. When entering into sponsorships agreements, it is important that both sides are committed to the relationship. Some sponsors, such as Red Bull and SteelSeries, actively promote E-Sports. Alienware, a technology company, provides products for E-Sports teams to use. Mobil 1, a motor oil brand, sponsors *Rocket League*, a game that is a mix of driving and soccer, showing the cross-over between the virtual world and reality.

INTELLECTUAL PROPERTY

When gaming companies like Blizzard, Valve, or Riot Games run their own tournaments and competitions, they set the ground rules concerning their own games. But problems arise when other entities sponsor tournaments using someone else's games. Such events are known as third-party tournaments. To what extent do gaming companies have a say in how their games are used by others, especially within professional gaming? This controversy has to do with intellectual property (IP).

An example of how the IP controversy affects society can be found in South Korea. Founded in 2000, the Korea E-Sports Association (KeSPA) was approved by their government's Ministry of Culture and Tourism. This backing encourages and promotes gaming throughout the country. South Korea remains a powerhouse in E-Sports, where it has created designated E-Sports stadiums. Additionally, competitive gaming as a leisure activity remains popular throughout the country.

In April 2010, news broke that Blizzard Entertainment was breaking partnership ties with KeSPA. Blizzard owns *StarCraft*, which has been widely popular in South Korea since its original release.

One sponsor of E-Sports tournaments is Alienware. It is a technology company that designs gaming products.

KeSPA sold the right to broadcast *StarCraft* to the International E-Sports/Entertainment Festival, which then licensed the rights to two other companies. Blizzard's senior director of Global Community Development and E-Sports said, "It's as if someone in Korea painted this amazing painting and then someone in the United States took . . . a digital version of that painting, made postcards and sold it without acknowledging the rights of the painter or giving them any kind of consideration. . . . We wouldn't think that that was fair."[41]

The IP issue can become complicated with so many different games created by a wide variety of companies being used within E-Sports and competitive gaming. The issue of IP rights will continue to arise as E-Sports gain even more prominence.

CHANGING STEREOTYPES

Within E-Sports, there is an ongoing debate between whether gamers are geeks or athletes, just as the debate rages about whether E-Sports is an actual sport. Whereas in previous generations, being a geek held negative connotations, it no longer holds the same meaning. For some professional gamers, being a geek or a nerd is part of their identity, and they choose to be identified as such. Researcher T.L. Taylor says, "For these players being a geek, or specifically a gaming geek, is a core component to their identity, in which pro gaming is simply a natural result of that passion."[42]

But for others, such as famed former professional gamer Johnathan "Fatal1ty" Wendel, there is no line dividing video games and athletics. In a 2006 interview, he said, "A lot of people have the stereotype that gamers sit behind computers all day, and of course we are sitting behind computers training and practicing. At the same time, most of us are athletes. We all played sports growing up because in the game we're using the same tactics, skills, and mindset to out-think and out-maneuver opponents."[43] In watching an E-Sports tournament today, viewers will witness a mix of those who align themselves in either the geek or athlete camp. Unlike traditional sports, there is no certain body

> **"A lot of people have the stereotype that gamers sit behind computers all day. . . . [M]ost of us are athletes. We all played sports growing up because in the game we're using the same tactics, skills, and mindset to out-think and out-maneuver opponents."[43]**
>
> *–Johnathan "Fatal1ty" Wendel, professional E-Sports player*

type or physical make-up giving a gamer an advantage over others. In the end, the victor is determined by video gaming skill alone.

One major disparity among today's E-Sports competitors is the major gap between the number of female and male gamers at all levels. When ordinary gamers are playing online games for fun at home, girls and women sometimes choose to hide their gender by turning off voice communication and picking gender neutral games. They do so in an attempt to avoid harassment from other players. However, professional E-Sports players have no such anonymous option. One researcher says, "These public gaming spaces have always been overly aggressive and masculinized and, as such, have often precluded participation by hesitant female gamers, who are often considered subpar or seeking attention before even having the chance to play."[44] This is not to say that women are not present in the world of E-Sports, but more often, they appear in the roles of interviewers and fans rather than the star gamers onstage.

Until 2014, the International E-Sports Federation (IESF) kept its tournaments segregated by men and women. When it opened all tournaments to women, it released a statement saying:

Female gamers make up half of the world's gaming population, but only a small percentage of E-Sports competitors are women. The IESF's female-only competitions aim to bring more diversity to competitive play by improving the representation of women at these events. Without efforts to improve representation, E-Sports can't achieve true gender equality.[45]

Today, there continue to be female participants both in major E-Sports tournaments and in women-only tournaments, but the overall number remains low. Ricki Ortiz is the only female team

Ricki Ortiz (left) is one of the few female professional E-Sports players. She plays fighting games as a member of the team Evil Geniuses.

member on Evil Geniuses. She also came out as transgender in 2014. Many E-Sports teams do not have any female players. The top earning female E-Sports player, Sasha "Scarlett" Hostyn, is a *StarCraft II* player. Ranked number 275 in the world, she more than doubled her 2017 earnings in 2018.

NEGATIVE BEHAVIORS IN GAMING

While the world of gaming is filled with well-meaning players, some are quickly recognized for bad behavior. Some communicate insults and slurs through chat capabilities. But, as one gamer notes, it is important to keep perspective: "They're just exploiting their anonymity. I know the person wouldn't say that to me in person. But their words don't really have power if they can't play the game."[46] Trolls are pranksters, the gamers who trick new players and create havoc on the playing field. Cheaters are those who pay others to make their character more powerful or unfairly gain useful items. They go to great lengths to avoid the hours dedicated players spend studying the game and slowly earning levels and powers. Griefing is the practice of purposely trying to make someone else's gaming experience miserable, such as by randomly attacking other players in the game with no purpose.

Some of today's biggest gaming controversies center around the practice of selling loot boxes and skins. Juniper Research explains, "Loot boxes are in-game packs which contain a random selection of items; while skins are in-game cosmetics which change the appearance of weapons or characters."[47] Loot boxes have a clear draw: if a player wants a certain item, the lure is to keep purchasing loot boxes until the item is obtained. There can be different tiers of loot boxes and cost depends on the game.

Skins are used as virtual currency which can later be cashed in for real money. Gamers acquire skins either through purchasing loot boxes or through playing games. Skins have value based on their rarity and popularity. "Issues arise where third-party websites facilitate wagering of skins on E-Sports matches and casino-style games; creating an unregulated gambling market," says Juniper's report.[48] This gambling is also being done by children, which is illegal. A 2017 study done in the United Kingdom found that 11 percent of eleven- to sixteen-year-olds had placed bets using skins. By 2022, Juniper says, the sale of loot boxes and skins gambling will reach $50 billion.

Other more direct forms of gambling within E-Sports have led to scandals. In 2015, a US *CS:GO* team, iBUYPOWER, intentionally lost a tournament to make money. One viewer who was part of the conspiracy placed bets that added up to $10,000 worth of *CS:GO* currency. The items won with the currency were then transferred back to the iBUYPOWER players. After the scandal was revealed, Valve banned the players from participating in any future Valve events.

Cheating by using performance-enhancing drugs such as Adderall is another recurring issue in E-Sports. Adderall is a stimulant used to treat ADHD. The drug can temporarily alter the brain to increase focus levels. In 2015, Kory "SEMPHIS" Friesen stated that he and his teammates used Adderall during a *CS:GO* tournament. This prompted the ESL to implement drug testing. Some players may need the drug for medical treatment, but others misuse it for a perceived advantage during competition. Issues surrounding performance-enhancing drugs continue to be studied by E-Sports authorities.

In response to these issues, the E-Sports Integrity Coalition was founded in July 2016 to promote fair play within E-Sports. With members from around the world, the group hopes to spread its key principles, such as the implementation of codes of conduct and investigations designed to prevent cheating, corruption, and drug use.

REGIONAL GAMING DIFFERENCES

The historical development of competitive gaming has differed between the Eastern and Western hemispheres. In the United States and throughout Europe, competitive gaming gained popularity through FPS games like *Doom* and *Quake*. Today, the FPS genre remains strong with *CS:GO, PUBG* and *Fortnite.*

In the East, E-Sports is centered in South Korea. In the 1990s, the South Korean government promoted the rapid growth of broadband infrastructure. Digital television and online gaming soon arrived to take

Players who spend hours perfecting their skills can be undermined by trolls and cheaters. This can lead players to lose games that they should have won.

advantage of the high-speed internet service. Whether for leisure or for competition, South Korean gamers tend to prefer MMORPGs and RTS games. Because of this, games such as Blizzard's *StarCraft* were immensely successful. *StarCraft* became so popular that TV stations broadcast competitive events. With the formation of the KeSPA, other countries started to follow their lead. Mike Morhaime witnessed E-Sports in South Korea before getting the idea to start BlizzCon in 2005. MMORPGs and RTS games continue to lead E-Sports in the Eastern hemisphere, though other genres have gained in popularity as well.

GAMING IN SCHOOL

College sports have long been a popular amateur form of sporting entertainment. Many fans enjoy watching not just professional football and basketball, but also the college teams of their hometown school. The same phenomenon has appeared in E-Sports. Robert Morris University, a college campus in Illinois, started varsity collegiate E-Sports in 2014. It offered scholarships to form a *League of Legends* team. Since that time, nearly seventy schools have started similar programs, and that number continues to rise. The National Association of Collegiate E-Sports (NACE) oversees the programs.

Heroes of the Dorm is a *Heroes of the Storm* tournament hosted by Blizzard. Started in 2015, the tournament has gained a following due to the grand prize: full college tuition. One former winner says, "You don't realize how much it means until it's the financial quarter and you don't have to pay. I'll never forget going back to school the next semester and being like, 'Oh, OK, I don't have to ask my parents for money.' That's when it really hit me."[49] At the 2018 Heroes of the Dorm, $500,000 in scholarship money and prizes were awarded. Open to any full-time college student in the United States or Canada, Heroes of the Dorm is rapidly growing.

The tournament mimics the NCAA basketball tournament, which is held around the same time of year. Hundreds of teams compete to gain entrance to a tournament of sixty-four. With the success of Heroes of the Dorm, other Blizzard titles such as *Hearthstone* and *StarCraft II* have been added to the schedule. A cofounder of the tournament says:

> We're at a point where a lot of universities are starting to
> directly invest in their teams by creating varsity programs,
> creating training facilities, hiring coaches. . . . I think overall

five years out we'll look at that and that'll be the norm, and
we'll have these programs on every major college campus in
North America.[50]

With the spreading prominence of E-Sports on college campuses, the next logical step is organized high school–level gaming. The High School Esports League (HSEL) was founded in 2012. Started by Mason Mullenioux and Charles Reilly shortly after their college graduations, HSEL works to bring E-Sports into the high schools. Mullenioux says, "There's a lot of older people who don't get it. But that's changing. With colleges starting to offer scholarships, varsity E-Sports will exist all over the country soon."[51]

Ryan Champlin received an E-Sports scholarship to attend college. He says people don't clearly understand the opportunities E-Sports has to offer, "There's marketing and management and coaching and recruiting. You can compose music or even be an announcer. You don't have to be great at games or even play to participate. There's animating and coding. There are so many ways for people to get involved and find a community."[52]

While some schools may be hesitant to incorporate E-Sports, James O'Hagan, founder of the Academy of E-Sports, notes that E-Sports is merely

> **"There's a lot of older people who don't get it. But that's changing. With colleges starting to offer scholarships, varsity E-Sports will exist all over the country soon."**[51]
>
> *–Mason Mullenioux, co-founder of the High School Esports League*

a "repackaged interest."[53] Students already have the drive to play competitive video games. When playing in organized groups, players can form a team and build relationships rather than gaming alone. Strategies and teamwork skills are rehearsed, and aerobic exercise is even incorporated to mentally prepare for matches.

This has opened new pathways to college for some students. With more and more colleges offering E-Sports scholarships, students who may have determined college was not their path are now taking a second look. O'Hagan also notes that gaming has other benefits, saying, "We've become so 'college and career ready' that we've forgotten about the importance of play."[54]

> **"We've become so 'college and career ready' that we've forgotten about the importance of play."** [54]
>
> *—James O'Hagan, Academy of E-Sports founder*

GAMING DISORDERS

In June 2018, the World Health Organization (WHO) announced a new classification under the category of disorders due to addictive behaviors: Gaming Disorder. According to the WHO's documents,

Gaming disorder is characterized by a pattern of persistent or recurrent gaming behaviour ('digital gaming' or 'video-gaming'), which may be online (i.e., over the internet) or offline, manifested by: 1) impaired control over gaming (e.g., onset, frequency, intensity, duration, termination, context); 2) increasing priority given to gaming to the extent that gaming takes precedence over other life interests and daily activities;

and 3) continuation or escalation of gaming despite the occurrence of negative consequences. The behaviour pattern is of sufficient severity to result in significant impairment in personal, family, social, educational, occupational or other important areas of functioning.[55]

The announcement was met with strong emotion on both sides of the issue. The WHO's Dr. Shekhar Saxena admits the classification may only pertain to an estimated 2 to 3 percent of gamers. Yet it is necessary to help those who do fit into this category get insurance coverage for needed medical assistance.

While the majority of gamers play for enjoyment, the small percentage who become addicted may have additional underlying medical issues such as depression. The point of the WHO's document is to raise awareness of an issue impacting global citizens and offer help to those who need it most. Those against the WHO's statement say the organization is basing its conclusions mainly from Asia, even though gaming is a global phenomenon.

A proclamation like that of the WHO may have a significant impact on those who hope to break into the professional scene of E-Sports. The difference between training to compete in a tournament and addictive behavior may be hard to define. The controversy also raises the issue of whether E-Sports is viewed as a real sport. Traditional athletes train multiple hours per day for upcoming meets and competitions. Holding them to the same standards and criteria, it may be hard to determine whether the athlete is addicted or merely highly competitive.

CHAPTER 4

THE FUTURE OF
E-SPORTS AND
COMPETITIVE GAMING

The future of E-Sports and competitive gaming will remain closely linked to advances in gaming technology and its spread around the globe. A 2018 movie gave a glimpse of what this future might look like. *Ready Player One*, based on a 2011 science-fiction novel, is set in 2045. The real world has become a harsh place, so Wade Watts and his friends escape to the popular virtual realm of the OASIS. When it is revealed that the game's founder has died and left a treasure hunt to determine who will inherit ownership of the OASIS, the real game begins. In 2018, this movie grossed over $580 million worldwide. Its science-fiction world may be far away. But virtual reality (VR) has already become a part of the gaming industry, and it is likely to have effects on E-Sports and competitive gaming.

TECHNOLOGICAL ADVANCES

SuperData notes that VR has become a major aspect of modern gaming: "The new cross-platform digital games landscape and the continued growth of new segments like E-Sports, gaming video content, and virtual reality have led to a dynamic market that shows

VR is shaping the future of video games. Soon E-Sports may feature VR games in tournaments.

no sign of slowing."[56] While VR is gaining momentum, it won't be mainstream until VR headsets are as readily available to people as smartphones are today. Devices like Facebook's Oculus Go headset, which do not require separate, expensive hardware to use, are aimed at making VR mainstream. A Seattle-area start-up, VRstudios, is a VR arcade where customers gather to experience VR much like previous generations went to an arcade to play the latest video games. VRstudios has installed 64 VRcade systems in 14 countries.

Another recent development in gaming technology is augmented reality (AR). AR provides a user with a composite view of the real world overlaid with computer generated images. *Pokémon Go*, a smartphone game in which players travel to real-world locations to capture specific types of monsters, is an example of AR. With its success, more games may take that direction. Tim Cook, the chief executive officer of technology company Apple, says AR "is going to change the way we use technology forever."[57] Research firm IDC predicts shipments of VR/AR headsets will expand quickly and increase to 68.9 million by 2022. As was true with the first computers, practical applications for VR/AR can be found in many major industries. They are already being used to create virtual classrooms, decorate homes, perform medical procedures, and assist with manufacturing. Once that groundwork is laid and pricing becomes more affordable, the games are likely to follow.

> **"[AR] is going to change the way we use technology forever."** [57]
>
> *–Tim Cook, Apple CEO*

Eye-tracking technology was spotlighted in the 2018 E-Sports *Street Fighter V* Invitational. A reporter says, "Fans will be able to see through the eyes of competitors as they fight for $250,000 in prize money."[58] Using micro-projectors and sensors, a visual map is created, allowing fans to view the game as the player sees it. Robert Occhialini of Turner Sports says, "As E-Sports continue to grow, technology presents unique opportunities for fans to have a window into the decision making of these highly skilled players."[59] Eye-tracking technology goes beyond live streaming. Over time, audiences will see how emerging technologies impact not only the gamers but also the viewing experience.

Additional ways to involve home viewers continue to develop. Twitch has announced a partnership with SLIVER.tv to include trivia questions as part of live-streamed broadcasts. This makes live streams more interactive. The trivia questions are geared toward the streamer and the game being streamed. Participants are rewarded for correct answers, and early statistics showed viewers who tried the trivia watched 40 percent longer. Twitch's popular streamer Erik "F10m" Flom says he is excited not only because of lengthened views, but because, "my viewers and the Bits [in-game currency] they use directly support me while participating in the trivia and competing for the top of the leaderboards. All you have to do is enable the extension and let the fun begin."[60] This will provide the streamer with added income as well as create heightened fan involvement.

Amazon, the owner of Twitch, recently announced a new service called GameOn. This is a service provided to gaming companies through Amazon. It intends to encourage amateur gaming by helping game developers run tournaments and competitions. The developers can offer in-game prizes, such as virtual currency, to competitors. But they can also offer real-world prizes by picking something from Amazon's website that is shipped directly to the winner.

MOBILE DEVICES VS. PERSONAL COMPUTERS

As the number of people with smartphones increases, so does the number of people using these devices for gaming. Newzoo reports, "In Asia, mobile E-Sports already has a similar structure to PC-based E-Sports franchises, with many top mobile competitive titles having professional leagues, live stadium events, and millions of viewers."[61] Experts expect this trend to continue in Asia. Newzoo expects the

Mobile device games also have loyal followings and large communities. Some popular E-Sports games such as Fortnite *can be played on mobile devices.*

North American E-Sports scene to remain largely PC-based, while mobile device gaming will remain a niche. Still, large communities do form around popular mobile games. *Clash Royale*, released in 2016, earns millions of dollars a month in revenue. It has a loyal following that participates in competitions on local levels.

WILL E-SPORTS PLAYERS UNIONIZE?

When an E-Sports player joins a team, he or she signs a contract. The contract spells out the relationship between the player, the teammates, and the team owner. It also explains how and when the player is paid and what expenses will be reimbursed. It may cover behavior expectations and the consequences of negative behavior. Contracts are meant to protect the rights of the players as well as those in charge of paying the players.

In many professional fields, including professional sports, the workers or players form unions. The purpose of a union is to protect the interests of the players and to act as representatives in negotiations, most often regarding working conditions or salary. But E-Sports players have not unionized. T.L. Taylor speculates this may be due to the age of many professional gamers. She says, "There is also the issue that many (especially young) players are often simply grateful to get any help or legitimacy in supporting their game play and so longer-term organization may feel out of step with their own thankfulness for any support at all."[62] Professional gaming careers are often short and of an undetermined length, making it difficult for unions to form and function. As E-Sports continues its explosive rise in popularity, players may eventually band together to form a union for the industry.

THE FUTURE OF WOMEN IN E-SPORTS

There are signs that the landscape of E-Sports may be shifting from male predominance. A 2017 study conducted by the E-Sports Ad Bureau and research firm Magid found that one in three E-Sports viewers are women. In addition, 78 percent of those women had just begun watching within the previous year. The study states, "Because of that, women could account for half of all growth in E-Sports viewership over the next year."[63]

Looking forward, those numbers could grow. Encouraged by South Korea's advanced E-Sports scene, *Overwatch* fans sometimes pack arenas in which men are the minority—though the women are fans, not players. The *Overwatch* hero character D.Va has sparked her own fan following and has been used by South Korean women to promote equality within South Korea.

In the United States, Stephens College in Columbia, Missouri, became the first all-women's college to have a varsity E-Sports program in 2017. Dianne Lynch, president of Stephens College, says, "Our mission is to ensure that women can succeed and can make choices about anything they do in any environment and in any profession. That's our mission. So why would we not do it in E-Sports?"[64]

The Stephens College Stars will be part of *Overwatch* leagues that compete in the Heroes of the Dorm series. *Overwatch* is popular not only because it is a well-made FPS, but also because of the game's message of diversity and inclusiveness.

> **"Our mission is to ensure that women can succeed and can make choices about anything they do in any environment and in any profession. That's our mission. So why would we not do it in E-Sports?"**[64]
>
> *–Dianne Lynch, president of Stephens College*

The cast of heroes that players can choose from represent a variety of ages, ethnicities, and genders. The gamers know they will face obstacles as an all-female team, but they hope to instill expectations of appropriate behavior and civility toward all players, male and female. Lynch says, "We're not naïve. We expect that there will be moments of difficulty—maybe lots of them. But at some point, women have always stood up and said, 'No, we're going to be a part of this. And you will, we will, be treated with the civility and respect we deserve.' Why should E-Sports be any different?"[65] With the loyal fans and educational institutions ready to support female gamers, the future face of E-Sports may be decidedly more female.

THE ROLE OF FANS

Chris Champlin, a former wrestler for Syracuse University, always loved video games. Playing Atari through childhood, he persisted in playing console games into adulthood. When Champlin became a parent, he encouraged his sons to play video games as well. So when Champlin's sons asked to attend a *CS:GO* tournament instead of a New York Jets game, he agreed. The boys returned from the tournament determined to bring E-Sports to their high school. Chris Champlin's son, Ryan, graduated with an E-Sports scholarship. This illustrates changing views as generations who grew up with video games encourage younger generations to pursue games professionally. It also shows how a passionate youngster can step up with an idea to change not only his future, but the future of other gamers.

Spectators have always been a part of the video game experience. While it may not be as exciting as controlling the game, spectators cheer and offer comments and suggestions. Because people are watching, gamers feel high levels of expectation to perform. Spectators help gamers understand their role as the professional player, creating a high level of expectation. Streaming is today's method of virtual spectatorship. With numbers continually expanding, this points to the consistent interest viewers will have in

Fans are what make the growth of E-Sports possible. Large fan turnouts at tournaments and sponsorships on services such as Twitch help people make E-Sports a career.

future years. New ways of interaction between fans and streamers will continue pushing the competitive gaming landscape forward.

Fans tend to follow one game or a genre of games that they play avidly. Fans are the driving factor behind the merchandising of E-Sports products. Taylor says fans "infuse energy into events, giving meaning and social importance to activities" and contribute through comments on social media and in the real world.[66] As E-Sports reaches global importance, its fans will positively impact the economics and the social communities connected to it.

PARENTAL VIEWS CHANGING

Chris Champlin encouraged his children because he grew up with a love of video games. But other parents are much more cautious about allowing their children to play for the lengths of time needed to become a professional gamer. Parents like Sumail Hassan's worry about the amount of time a child spends playing video games to the exclusion of other social activities or homework. Even if a person excels at competitive gaming, his or her parents may be hesitant about supporting this career path.

Kim Price, mother of Dillon Price—a gamer known as "Attach" to *Call of Duty* fans—explains, "We kept quiet about the fact that Dillon competed playing video games. Only a few family members knew he played. At the time they were concerned with the impact his gaming would have on his grades."[67] When Dillon started winning, people's views changed. Kim Price offers this suggestion to players, "I would say to them first take care of school and family responsibilities because those are absolute priority."[68] For parents, she says:

> *My advice would be to attend events and meet the other parents. I always look forward to and have enjoyed meeting some of the parents at the tournaments I've attended. . . . I think it's so important to support and cheer our kids on. . . . If you become interested in your child's interests, that becomes so empowering for them.*[69]

With the quick expansion of E-Sports in the high school and college realms, parents are becoming more aware of the monetary benefits to competitive gaming. Thus, they want their children to succeed and become the best gamers possible. In 2018, the *Wall Street Journal* reported that parents of elementary and middle school students paid tutors to help their children improve at *Fortnite*.

Reporter Sarah E. Needleman said, "Winning bestows the kind of bragging rights that used to be reserved for the local Little League baseball champ. Just like eager dugout dads opening their wallets for pitching lessons, videogame parents are more than willing to pay for their offspring to gain an edge."[70] Dedicated to coaching and training all levels of gamers and E-Sports athletes, the website Gamer Sensei was founded in 2016. Gamers can choose a coach based on teacher profiles, preferred games, or even time zones. A trend of hiring E-Sports coaches may signal a shift in parenting style that will continue as older gamers become parents and begin to raise the next generation of gamers.

ECONOMIC AND CORPORATE IMPACT

Research agency Statista reported that in 2010, $3 million in prize money was awarded in E-Sports tournaments. An increasing trend year by year brought the total to $121 million by 2017. Increasing sponsorships, coverage of events, and notoriety of professional players should continue to widen the viewership of E-Sports and therefore add to the ever-growing prize pools awarded at tournaments.

With Asia and North America representing the two largest E-Sports markets, global revenue increases over the last several years have seen 40 percent growth. If that rate continues, US E-Sports revenue will be $1.5 billion by 2020. This will enable developers and companies to continue to expand and experiment with new games and technologies in an ever-changing gaming landscape.

In December 2017, computer processing giant Intel announced a partnership with ESL. Through this partnership, Intel would provide the latest technology for teams and players, sponsor the Intel Extreme Masters, a global E-Sports event, and sponsor designated

THE GLOBALIZATION OF E-SPORTS

E-Sports viewers in the United States already outnumber National Hockey League viewers, and E-Sports are expected to also surpass Major League Baseball in viewership. Outside the United States, the growth is even more rapid. When games-related research firm Newzoo started in 2009, it followed E-Sports in six countries. By 2018, that number had increased to twenty-eight countries. A great deal of growth has come in China, where many millions of people have joined the global gaming community. But increased exposure is spreading to Latin America, the Middle East, and Africa. This is due to improved infrastructure. As infrastructure improves, the interconnectedness among the world's continents—and their gamers—will improve too.

E-Sports arenas. The Intel Grand Slam injected excitement by offering a bonus of $1,000,000 to any *CS:GO* team that could be the first to win four out of ten major tournaments. Promotions like this provide new reasons for players to compete. A senior vice president of Intel, Gregory Bryant, says, "Intel's involvement in E-Sports and the gaming community has spanned more than 15 years, and we're always looking for ways to take the player and fan experience to the next level."[71]

Before the 2018 PyeongChang Winter Olympics, Intel held an Intel Extreme Masters tournament, IEM PyeongChang. The event featured Blizzard's *StarCraft II*, and it drew massive crowds to the Olympic town. Bryant says, "Our goal is to bring E-Sports to every global sporting stage. From the qualifying events to the groundbreaking Intel Extreme Masters tournament in PyeongChang, we see this as another important step in giving more people around the world a chance to experience the thrill of E-Sports."[72] Not only were tourists, athletes, and families able to observe the tournament, but the International Olympic Committee (IOC) was invited to observe as well.

E-Sports was a demonstration sport at the 2018 Asian Games. In 2022, E-Sports gamers will be able to compete in the games for a medal.

E-SPORTS IN THE OLYMPICS

In 2018, E-Sports debuted at the Asian Games as a demonstration sport. This means it was being considered for future addition to the list of sport competitions that were already a part of the games. Like the Olympics, the Asian Games are held every four years. These games bring together athletes from across the Asian continent to compete for medals. As reported by the *League of Legends* website, "The [Asian Games] event is recognized by the International Olympic Committee as the second largest multi-sport event after the Olympics."[73]

By 2022, E-Sports will be an official medal sport of the Asian Games, scheduled to be held in Hangzhou, China, that year. This means medals will be awarded to the winners. Looking forward, there are talks of E-Sports being added to the 2024 Olympic Games in Paris. The IOC officially recognized E-Sports as a sport in late 2017, an important first step in entering the games. If E-Sports is part of the Paris Games, it would be as a demonstration sport. The IESF's Secretary General, Leopold Chung, says, "There are great engagement numbers,

> **"There are great engagement numbers, great fan numbers in France, especially in Paris, who would definitely want to come to an E-Sports game." [74]**
>
> *—Leopold Chung, The International E-Sports Federation's Secretary General*

great fan numbers in France, especially in Paris, who would definitely want to come to an E-Sports game."[74] Beyond Paris, the IOC's acknowledgement of E-Sports shows that it is aware of E-Sports's popularity, especially among younger audiences. To make the Olympics relevant to new generations, it may be in the IOC's best interest to make E-Sports an official Olympic game.

There is no denying the rise of E-Sports around the world and its impact on culture globally. As internet access and digital technologies spread, societies will continue to use them to communicate, work, and play. Video games, with their competitive lure, are likely to resonate with new audiences. Communities will form and grow around games as people continue searching for competitive outlets in an increasingly virtual world.

SOURCE NOTES

INTRODUCTION: GAMING AS A JOB

1. Team Liquid, "Liquid Dota | TI7 Champions," *YouTube*, August 12, 2017. www.youtube.com.

2. "Liquid Wins the International 2017," *Team Liquid*, August 13, 2017. www.teamliquidpro.com.

3. "Market Brief—2017 Digital Games and Interactive Media Year in Review," *SuperData Research*, 2018. www.superdataresearch.com.

4. Ethan Cloute, Communication with Author, May 25, 2018.

5. Esports Stories, "The Story of SumaiL | Syed Sumail Hassan | Evil Geniuses | Dota 2 | Biography | Profile," *YouTube*, March 12, 2017. www.youtube.com.

6. Quoted in Guinness World Records, *Guinness World Records 2018 Gamer's Edition: The Ultimate Guide to Gaming Records*. London, England: Guinness World Records, p. 22.

7. Quoted in Noah Smith, "Esports Training Facility Brings Gaming Another Step Closer to Traditional Pro Sports," *Washington Post*, May 10, 2018. www.washingtonpost.com.

CHAPTER 1: THE HISTORY OF COMPETITIVE GAMING

8. Quoted in Andrew Ervin, *Bit by Bit: How Video Games Transformed Our World*. New York: Basic Books, 2017, p. 17.

9. Quoted in David Friedman, "Inventor Portrait," *NPR*, December 8, 2014, www.npr.org.

10. Ethan Gilsdorf, *Fantasy Freaks and Gaming Geeks*. Lanham, MD: Lyons Press, 2009, p. 72.

11. Gilsdorf, *Fantasy Freaks and Gaming Geeks*, p. 187.

12. Quoted in Ervin, *Bit by Bit*, p. 76.

13. Steven L. Kent, *The Ultimate History of Video Games: The Story Behind the Craze That Touched Our Lives and Changed the World*. New York: Three Rivers Press, 2001, p. 116.

14. Quoted in Kent, *The Ultimate History of Video Games*, p. 141.

15. Quoted in Rusel DeMaria and Johnny L. Wilson, *High Score: The Illustrated History of Electronic Games*. New York: McGraw-Hill, 2004.

16. Quoted in Mark J. P. Wolf, ed., *Before the Crash: Early Video Game History*. Detroit, MI: Wayne State UP, 2012, p. 149.

17. Quoted in DeMaria and Wilson, *High Score: The Illustrated History of Electronic Games*, p. 270.

18. Quoted in Blizzard Entertainment, "StarCraft Is Life: A 20th Anniversary Celebration," *StarCraft II Official Game Site*, April 9, 2018. www.starcraft2.com.

19. Quoted in Dave Oliver, "Mike Morhaime on 20 Years of StarCraft E-Sports," *StarCraft II Official Game Site*, March 4, 2018, www.starcraft2.com.

CHAPTER 2: HOW DO PEOPLE PLAY E-SPORTS?

20. T.L. Taylor, *Raising the Stakes: E-Sports and the Professionalization of Computer Gaming*. Cambridge, MA: MIT Press, 2012, p. 99.

21. Taylor, *Raising the Stakes*, p. 88.

22. Ethos, "Nearly 70% of Gamers Want a Better Way to Play Competitive Online Games," *Ethos*, n.d. www.ethos.gg.

23. Taylor, *Raising the Stakes*, p. 94.

24. Clinton Loomis, *Free to Play*, produced by Valve (2014; San Francisco, CA: Valve, 2014). Film.

25. Clinton Loomis, Twitter Post, May 27, 2018, 3:20 PM. www.twitter.com.

26. "Average Age in E-Sports vs. Major Sports," *ESPN*, September 20, 2017. www.espn.com.

27. Quoted in *Free to Play*, 2014.

28. "Free 2018 Global ESPORTS Market Report," *Newzoo*, p. 25. www.resources.newzoo.com.

29. "Market Brief—2017 Digital Games and Interactive Media Year in Review."

30. "Free 2018 Global ESPORTS Market Report."

31. Ethan Cloute, Communication with Author, May 25, 2018.

32. Julia Alexander, "Fortnite's Pro-Am Tournament Embraced a New Type of Video Game God," *Polygon*, June 14, 2018. www.polygon.com.

33. Quoted in Smith, "Esports Training Facility Brings Gaming Another Step Closer to Traditional Pro Sports."

34. Quoted in Smith, "Esports Training Facility Brings Gaming Another Step Closer to Traditional Pro Sports."

35. Quoted in Taylor, *Raising the Stakes*, pp. 225–231.

36. Lol Esports, "Closer Look: Referees in the LCS," *YouTube*, March 21, 2015. www.youtube.com.

CHAPTER 3: HOW DO E-SPORTS AFFECT SOCIETY?

37. "Market Brief—2017 Digital Games and Interactive Media Year in Review."

38. "Pro Gamer Tyler 'Ninja' Blevins Smashes Records with Fortnite Streams," *CNBC*, March 19, 2018. www.cnbc.com.

39. "Free 2018 Global ESPORTS Market Report."

40. Xen Chalmet, *Sponsorship Within eSports: Examining the Sponsorship Relationship Quality Constructs*. Gothenburg, Sweden: University of Gothenburg School of Business, Economics and Law, 2015, p. 7.

41. Quoted in Taylor, *Raising the Stakes*, pp. 163–166.

42. Taylor, *Raising the Stakes*, p. 115.

43. Forbes, "Playing Video Games for a Living," *YouTube*, May 25, 2006. www.youtube.com.

44. Michael Borowy and Dal Yong Jin, "Pioneering E-Sport: The Experience Economy and the Marketing of Early 1980s Arcade Gaming Contests," *International Journal of Communication*, 2013, pp. 2254–2274.

45. Quoted in Phil Savage, "IeSF Removes Male-Only Restriction from Its E-Sports Tournaments," *PC Gamer*, July 3, 2014. www.pcgamer.com.

46. Ethan Cloute, Communication with Author, May 25, 2018.

47. "Juniper Research: Loot Boxes & Skins Gambling to Generate a $50 Billion Industry by 2022," *E-Sports Marketing Blog*, May 30, 2018. www.esports-marketing-blog.com.

48. "Juniper Research: Loot Boxes & Skins Gambling."

49. Quoted in Sean Morrison, "As Heroes of the Dorm 'Graduates,' Former Players and Admins Reflect on Success," *ESPN*, May 10, 2018. www.espn.com.

50. Quoted in Morrison, "As Heroes of the Dorm 'Graduates.'"

51. Quoted in David Gardner, "Forget Friday Night Lights, Esports Is Becoming the Next Varsity Obsession," *Bleacher Report*, 2018. www.bleacherreport.com.

52. Quoted in Gardner, "Forget Friday Night Lights."

53. Vicki Davis, "James O'Hagan: 5 Reasons to Bring ESports to Your School," *The 10-Minute Teacher Show with Vicki Davis, the Cool Cat Teacher*, May 11, 2018. www.10minuteteacher.libsyn.com.

54. Davis, "James O'Hagan: 5 Reasons to Bring ESports to Your School."

55. World Health Organization, "6C51 Gaming Disorder," *ICD-11 for Mortality and Morbidity Statistics*, 2018. www.icd.who.int.

CHAPTER 4: THE FUTURE OF E-SPORTS AND COMPETITIVE GAMING

56. "Market Brief—2017 Digital Games and Interactive Media Year in Review."

57. Quoted in Dawn C. Chmielewski, "Apple's Tim Cook Says Augmented Reality Will 'Change Everything,'" *Deadline Hollywood*, November 2, 2017. www.deadline.com.

58. Nicole Carpenter, "Pro Player Eye Movements Will Be Tracked During the ELEAGUE Street Fighter 5 Invitational," *Dot Esports*, May 31, 2018. www.dotesports.com.

59. Quoted in Carpenter, "Pro Player Eye Movements."

60. Quoted in David Hollingsworth, "Twitch Partners with SLIVER.tv to Launch Interactive Trivia Extension," *Esports Insider*, April 24, 2018. www.esportsinsider.com.

61. "Free 2018 Global ESPORTS Market Report."

62. Taylor, *Raising the Stakes*, pp. 178–179.

63. Nicole Carpenter, "Report: Women Make Up Nearly One-Third of E-Sports Viewers," *Dot Esports*, June 20, 2017. www.dotesports.com.

64. Quoted in Sean Morrison, "Rising Stars: All-Women's Stephens College Breaks Ground with Varsity E-Sports Program," *ESPN*, April 20, 2017. www.espn.com.

65. Quoted in Morrison, "Rising Stars."

66. Taylor, *Raising the Stakes*, pp. 184–186.

67. "Pro Gaming Parents—Interview with Attach's Mom," *Dexerto*, May 16, 2016. www.dexerto.com.

68. "Pro Gaming Parents—Interview with Attach's Mom."

69. "Pro Gaming Parents—Interview with Attach's Mom."

70. Sarah E. Needleman, "Ready, Aim, Hire a 'Fortnite' Coach: Parents Enlist Videogame Tutors for Their Children," *Wall Street Journal*, July 31, 2018. www.wsj.com.

71. Quoted in Hans Oelschlagel, "Intel and ESL Announce Biggest Multi-event Deal in E-Sports History," *ESL Gaming*, December 6, 2017, www.eslgaming.com.

72. Quoted in Patrick Garren, "Intel Announces IEM Pyeong Chang, with Support from the International Olympic Committee," *E-Sports Observer*, November 4, 2017. www.esportsobserver.com.

73. "League of Legends Selected as One of the Esports Titles for 2018 Asian Games," *Riot Games*, May 15, 2018. www.lolesports.com.

74. Quoted in Jack Tarrant, "Esports in Talks with Paris 2024 Over Demonstration Event," *Reuters*, April 25, 2018. www.reuters.com.

FOR FURTHER RESEARCH

BOOKS

Roland Li, *Good Luck Have Fun: The Rise of eSports*. New York: Skyhorse Publishing, 2016.

Laura Roberts, *Careers in Gaming*. San Diego, CA: ReferencePoint Press, 2017.

T.L. Taylor, *Raising the Stakes: E-Sports and the Professionalization of Computer Gaming*. Cambridge, MA: MIT Press, 2015.

Carolyn Williams-Noren, *Video Games and Culture*. San Diego, CA: ReferencePoint Press, 2019.

INTERNET SOURCES

Patrick Garren, "Intel Announces IEM Pyeong Chang, with Support from the International Olympic Committee," *E-Sports Observer*, November 4, 2017. www.esportsobserver.com.

Sean Morrison, "Rising Stars: All-Women's Stephens College Breaks Ground with Varsity E-Sports Program," *ESPN*, April 20, 2017. www.espn.com.

Sarah E. Needleman, "Ready, Aim, Hire a Fortnite Coach: Parents Enlist Videogame Tutors for Their Children," *Wall Street Journal*, July 31, 2018. www.wsj.com.

Luke Plunkett, "The Injuries That Are Ending E-Sports Careers," *Kotaku*, July 16, 2015. www.kotaku.com.

"Top Players of 2018," *E-Sports Earnings*, n.d. www.esportsearnings.com.

RELATED ORGANIZATIONS AND WEBSITES

International E-Sports Federation

www.ie-sf.org

The International E-Sports Federation (IESF) works to standardize E-Sports and get it recognized as a legitimate sport. Its website includes information about its goals, including organizing tournaments and meetings.

National Association of Collegiate E-Sports

1200 Grand Blvd.
Kansas City, MO 64106
www.nacesports.org

The National Association of Collegiate E-Sports (NACE) is a nonprofit organization formed by colleges and universities to encourage E-Sports on the collegiate level. It helps teams become eligible for collegiate competitions and awards scholarships to players

Twitch

www.twitch.tv

Twitch is one of the world's top destinations for watching streaming E-Sports and competitive gaming.

World Health Organization

1211 Geneva 27, Switzerland
www.who.int

The World Health Organization (WHO) is an international health organization that studies issues that affect public health, such as gaming disorder and video game addiction.

INDEX

INDEX CONTINUED

IMAGE CREDITS

ABOUT THE AUTHOR

Heather L. Bode has been writing non-fiction for more than fifteen years. With a focus on the magazine market as well as education, she has published more than one hundred articles, teacher's guides, and lesson plans. She lives in Montana with her husband and five children.